Your Journey Within

Within

"Weekly Affirmations"

**For Daily Success in Your
Business and the Workplace**

Chris Chaney

1

Ch.1: Introduction
Ch.2: The Power Behind Affirmations
Ch.3: Thriving Ventures
Ch.4: Pinnacle Progress
Ch.5: Wealthy Enterprises
Ch.6: Prosperous Horizons
Ch.7: Unified Energies
Ch.8: Connective Bonds
Ch.9: Professional Ascendance
Ch.10: Career Ascent
Ch.11: Rising Professional
Ch.12: Tranquil Proficiency
Ch.13: Business Flourish
Ch.14: Self-Enrichment Journey
Ch.15: Unified Strength
Ch.16: Cultivating Change
Ch.17: Serene Investments
Ch.18: Leadership Evolution
Ch.19: Career Mastery
Ch.20: Unleashing Potential
Ch.21: Innovative Ventures
Ch.22: Innovative Synergy
Ch.23: Conclusion

Chapter 1

Introduction

Hey, What's up?! I'm Chris. I want to personally thank you for taking time out to grab this book and join us on a journey of business and workplace growth, discovery, and development.

I understand firsthand how difficult things can get in business and how important it is to have positive self-talk.

I remember when I went flat broke in the summer of 2021. Yep, that's right, I was flat-out broke. I ran completely out of money and had to rely on my great aunt and uncle to help pay my payroll in my business along with the rent for my apartment.

I remember thinking to myself, "Chris, you know how you got here, you know how to get out, but it's going to start with the conversations you have with yourself." You see, ego is a b*tch sometimes and ego can make you think about things from a perspective that is simply just not beneficial for your growth.

I had decisions to make. What self-defeating thoughts and emotions would I listen to? What words would I use to dictate to my circumstances that would steer me out of this rut?

What I realized was this. The brain isn't designed to make you rich, successful, or happy. It's designed to keep you safe.

When you decide that your success in life hinges on the fact that you have to learn how to walk on water, alarm bells will blare in your head.

That's when it's time to connect to the right affirmations to get you through the fog of doubt and fear to move you closer to your next level.

Unlike the affirmations for your personal life, these affirmations are designed to quail your anxieties in the workplace. Whether you're a gig worker, solopreneur, business owner, or professional in the workplace, this book of affirmations is absolutely for you.

Let's conquer together. Why? Because we are stronger together.

Chapter 2

<u>The Power Behind Affirmations</u>

For ages, philosophers, self-help gurus, religious teachers, and artists have been discussing the power of affirmations. René Descartes said, "I think, therefore I Am". Moses in answering the Pharaoh's question as to who sent him said, "I Am". Even the rap artist Eminem said, "I Am whatever you say I Am, if I wasn't why would I say I Am."

The question then looms, if positive affirmations work so well, then why isn't everyone using them to excel in their lives?

The simple answer is, that they don't feel like their affirmations work. An even simpler answer is, that the self-talk that is working in their lives is the self-talk in which they're emotionally attached.

You see, the words alone mean nothing. Think about it, people say stuff all the time with absolutely no meaning or follow through. The words that count come with action and energy in motion produces action every time. Now, don't miss what you just read. Emotions cause actions. Emotionless affirmations will fall flat every single time you say it. The key to the affirmations in this book, in your journal, or anywhere is how you genuinely feel about what you're saying.

Another component of an affirmation that works s its ability to encompass past, present, and future tense. For example, let's take "I Am". If I asked, were you the person that bought my book? Your answer would be, "I Am". If I was to ask, are you the person reading my book? Your answer would be, "I Am". Lastly, if I were to ask, are you a different person after reading this book? Your answer would hopefully be, "I am".   7

We compiled seven phases to create an affirmation for each day. Those phrases are: "I Am", "I Have", "I Feel", "I See", "I Speak", "I Do", and "I Create." Those seven phrases are designed to create the feeling of excitement, anticipation, expectation, determination, and confidence.

Let's get back to the brain for a second. When you can create feelings of excitement, anticipation, expectation, determination, and confidence in your mind and body something magical happens. The brain will create a neurological connection between your affirmation, your thoughts, and feelings that create what I call a "Future Memory".

Since the limbic brain cannot tell the difference between fact and fiction, when you create "Future Memories", you've created a "future past" experience that will turn on your reticular activating system.   8

Turning on your reticular activating system will allow you to see and experience in your environment the very affirmations that you are affirming.

Hey, I'm excited to be a part of this amazing journey with you. I'm excited to see your growth and look forward to hearing from you when you see the manifestation of your goals and affirmations.

Before you get started let's touch bases on a few techniques that you can use to maximize the affirmations in this book.

You can read the book the book straight through if you like. You'll get a different subject for your affirmation each week. Or, you can pick your favorite weeks and turn those into sort of a mantra of affirmations. You can mix and match your affirmations. I want you to be creative and have fun with your experience with this book.   9

Also, last thing. I'm a huge fan of journaling. I encourage you to journal while you're affirming. Grab a journal from the store or you grab the accompanying journal to this book. It's called, The Journey Within "Where, Why, What" Goal Journal. It's available on Amazon now.

Chapter 3

Thriving Ventures: A Week of Affirmations for Business Success

Monday (I Am):
I am a confident and capable entrepreneur, ready to navigate the path to business success.

Tuesday (I Have):
I have the skills and resources to lead my business towards unprecedented success.

Wednesday (I Feel):
I feel the energy of prosperity and growth infusing every aspect of my business.

Thursday (I See):
I see challenges as opportunities, driving my business towards greater success.

Friday (I Speak):
I speak words of innovation and resilience, fostering a thriving business mindset.

Saturday (I Do):
I actively engage in strategic actions that propel my business toward continuous success.

Sunday (I Create):
I create a vision for my business that aligns with success, laying the foundation for prosperity.

May this week of affirmations bring forth success and abundance in your business

Chapter 4

Pinnacle Progress: A Week of Affirmations for Elevating Business Growth

Monday (I Am):
I am the driving force behind my business's ascent, propelling it towards unparalleled growth.

Tuesday (I Have):
I have the acumen and resources to nurture and sustain continuous business growth.

Wednesday (I Feel):
I feel the momentum building, igniting a sense of excitement as my business expands.

Thursday (I See):
I see my business reaching new heights, with each challenge presenting an opportunity for growth.

Friday (I Speak):
I speak words of prosperity and abundance, cultivating a mindset conducive to business growth.

Saturday (I Do):
I actively engage in strategic initiatives that fuel the ongoing growth and success of my business.

Sunday (I Create):
I create an environment that fosters innovation and prosperity, paving the way for sustained business growth.

May this week of affirmations guide you toward the pinnacle of success and growth in your business ventures.

Chapter 5

<u>Wealthy Enterprises</u>: A Week of Affirmations for Seizing Investment Opportunities

Monday (I Am):
I am a wise and discerning investor, ready to explore and seize lucrative opportunities.

Tuesday (I Have):
I have the financial acumen and resources to make informed and successful investments.

Wednesday (I Feel):
I feel a sense of excitement and readiness to embrace profitable investment opportunities.

Thursday (I See):
I see opportunities where others might see challenges, unlocking the potential for prosperous investments.

Friday (I Speak):
I speak words of confidence and insight, attracting fruitful investment opportunities my way.

Saturday (I Do):
I actively engage in research and strategic actions that lead to successful investment ventures.

Sunday (I Create):
I create a mindset of abundance and discernment, opening doors to new and rewarding investment opportunities.

May this week of affirmations guide you toward fruitful and prosperous investment ventures.

Chapter 6

Prosperous Horizons: A Week of Affirmations for Embracing Business Opportunities

Monday (I Am):
I am a perceptive entrepreneur, tuned into the endless possibilities of business opportunities.

Tuesday (I Have):
I have the skills and insight to recognize and capitalize on lucrative business opportunities.

Wednesday (I Feel):
I feel a wave of optimism and readiness to seize the diverse business opportunities around me.

Thursday (I See):
I see doors opening to new business horizons, presenting valuable opportunities for growth.

Friday (I Speak):
I speak words of innovation and adaptability, attracting a flow of promising business opportunities.

Saturday (I Do):
I actively engage in actions that position me to take full advantage of emerging business opportunities.

Sunday (I Create):
I create a mindset of abundance and receptivity, opening the path to unforeseen and prosperous business opportunities.

May this week of affirmations guide you toward a journey filled with diverse and rewarding business opportunities.

Chapter 7

Unified Energies: A Week of Affirmations
for Creating Harmony in the Workplace

Monday (I Am):
I am a source of positive energy,
contributing to the harmonious atmosphere
in the workplace.

Tuesday (I Have):
I have the ability to foster collaboration and
understanding, building a foundation for
workplace harmony.

Wednesday (I Feel):
I feel a sense of unity and cooperation,
creating a harmonious environment for
everyone.

19

Thursday (I See):
I see the strengths in each team member, appreciating the diverse contributions that enrich workplace harmony.

Friday (I Speak):
I speak words of encouragement and support, promoting open communication and unity in the workplace.

Saturday (I Do):
I actively engage in actions that nurture teamwork and cultivate a culture of harmony at work.

Sunday (I Create):
I create a workplace environment where harmony thrives, fostering a positive and collaborative spirit.

May this week of affirmations contribute to a workplace filled with unity, collaboration, and lasting harmony.

Chapter 8

Connective Bonds: A Week of Affirmations for Strengthening Workplace Relationships

Monday (I Am):
I am a positive force in building meaningful workplace connections, fostering a sense of camaraderie.

Tuesday (I Have):
I have the capacity to create authentic and supportive relationships with my colleagues.

Wednesday (I Feel):
I feel a genuine connection with my coworkers, promoting a harmonious workplace environment.

Thursday (I See):
I see the value in each team member, appreciating the unique contributions they bring to our workplace.

Friday (I Speak):
I speak words of encouragement and respect, nurturing positive and effective workplace relationships.

Saturday (I Do):
I actively engage in actions that strengthen and build trust within workplace relationships.

Sunday (I Create):
I create an atmosphere of collaboration and mutual support, enhancing the quality of workplace relationships.

May this week of affirmations contribute to the creation of strong and positive workplace relationships.   22

Chapter 9

<u>Professional Ascendance</u>: A Week of Affirmations for Job Growth

Monday (I Am):
I am a dynamic professional, attracting opportunities for growth and advancement in my career.

Tuesday (I Have):
I have the skills and capabilities to excel in my current role and embrace new opportunities for job growth.

Wednesday (I Feel):
I feel the energy of progress and advancement, propelling me toward substantial job growth.

Thursday (I See):
I see challenges as stepping stones to elevate my career, creating pathways for continuous job growth.

Friday (I Speak):
I speak words of ambition and competence, aligning my thoughts with a trajectory of job growth.

Saturday (I Do):
I actively engage in actions that contribute to my professional development and stimulate job growth.

Sunday (I Create):
I create a vision for my career that manifests in tangible job growth, paving the way for success.

May this week of affirmations guide you toward significant and fulfilling job growth in your professional journey.

Chapter 10

Career Ascent: A Week of Affirmations for Continuous Job Growth

Monday (I Am):
I am a proactive learner, consistently adapting and growing to unlock new dimensions of job opportunities.

Tuesday (I Have):
I have the determination to navigate challenges, propelling me toward sustained and meaningful job growth.

Wednesday (I Feel):
I feel a surge of confidence and readiness, embracing each workday as an opportunity for personal and professional advancement.

Thursday (I See):
I see every task as a chance to showcase my skills and contribute to the ongoing success and job growth in my career.

Friday (I Speak):
I speak words of ambition and perseverance, fostering an environment conducive to continuous job growth.

Saturday (I Do):
I actively engage in projects and initiatives that pave the way for job growth, aligning my efforts with career aspirations.

Sunday (I Create):
I create a strategic plan for my professional journey, ensuring a trajectory of sustained and rewarding job growth.

May this week of affirmations inspire and guide you toward continuous growth and success in your career.

Chapter 11

<u>Rising Professional</u>: A Week of
Affirmations for Promotion and Elevation

Monday (I Am):
I am deserving of career advancement, and
I embrace the potential for promotion with
confidence.

Tuesday (I Have):
I have accumulated valuable skills and
experiences, positioning myself for
promotion and elevation.

Wednesday (I Feel):
I feel a sense of readiness and excitement
for the challenges that come with career
promotion.

Thursday (I See):
I see myself reaching new heights in my career, visualizing the positive impact of promotion and elevation.

Friday (I Speak):
I speak words of ambition and success, fostering an atmosphere conducive to professional growth.

Saturday (I Do):
I actively engage in actions that demonstrate my capabilities and readiness for promotion.

Sunday (I Create):
I create a roadmap for career ascent, ensuring a journey of continuous promotion and elevation.

May this week of affirmations propel you toward the heights of professional success through promotion and elevation.

28

Chapter 12

Tranquil Proficiency: A Week of Affirmations for Cultivating a Stress-Free Workp ace

Monday (I Am):
I am a calming presence, contributing to the creation of a stress-free environment in the workplace.

Tuesday (I Have):
I have the ability to manage challenges with grace, promoting serenity throughout the workplace.

Wednesday (I Feel):
I feel a sense of tranquility within myself and radiate that peace to others in the workplace.

Thursday (I See):
I see opportunities to alleviate stress, fostering a positive and supportive workplace culture.

Friday (I Speak):
I speak words of encouragement and understanding, creating an atmosphere of stress-free collaboration.

Saturday (I Do):
I actively engage in activities that promote well-being and stress relief for myself and colleagues.

Sunday (I Create):
I create a workplace where harmony prevails, ensuring a stress-free and productive environment.

May this week of affirmations contribute to a workplace filled with tranquility, support, and freedom from unnecessary stress.   30

Chapter 13

Business Flourish: A Week of Affirmations for a Thriving Business

Monday (I Am):
I am a driving force behind the prosperity of my business, infusing it with energy and innovation.

Tuesday (I Have):
I have the skills and wisdom to navigate challenges and steer my business toward continuous growth.

Wednesday (I Feel):
I feel the pulse of success running through my business, fostering an environment of thriving growth.

Thursday (I See):
I see opportunities for expansion and prosperity, guiding my business toward new heights.

Friday (I Speak):
I speak words of abundance and success, manifesting a thriving atmosphere within my business.

Saturday (I Do):
I actively engage in actions that contribute to the continuous thriving and evolution of my business.

Sunday (I Create):
I create a vision for my business that aligns with prosperity, ensuring a path of sustained thriving.

May this week of affirmations bring forth a thriving and flourishing journey for your business.

Chapter 14

<u>Self-Enrichment Journey</u>: A Week of Affirmations for Investing In Yourself

Monday (I Am):
I am my greatest asset, recognizing the value in investing time and energy into my personal growth.

Tuesday (I Have):
I have the resources within me to invest in my skills, knowledge, and overall well-being.

Wednesday (I Feel):
I feel the empowerment that comes with self-investment, nurturing a positive and resilient mindset.

Thursday (I See):
I see opportunities for personal growth and development, making conscious choices to invest in myself.

Friday (I Speak):
I speak words of encouragement and self-empowerment, creating a mindset focused on continuous self-investment.

Saturday (I Do):
I actively engage in activities that contribute to my personal growth, investing in my talents and passions.

Sunday (I Create):
I create a path of self-enrichment, embracing the journey of investing in myself for a fulfilling life.

May this week of affirmations inspire and guide you on a transformative journey of investing in yourself.

Chapter 15

Unified Strength: A Week of Affirmations for Effective Team Building.

Monday (I Am):
I am a cornerstone of teamwork, contributing my unique strengths to the collective success.

Tuesday (I Have):
I have the ability to foster collaboration, creating an environment conducive to effective team building.

Wednesday (I Feel):
I feel a sense of unity within the team, strengthening our collective resolve for shared goals.

Thursday (I See):
I see the potential in each team member, appreciating diverse contributions that enhance team building.

Friday (I Speak):
I speak words of encouragement and camaraderie, nurturing a positive and supportive team culture.

Saturday (I Do):
I actively engage in team-building activities that strengthen bonds and enhance collaboration.

Sunday (I Create):
I create a team spirit that thrives on unity, fostering a culture of success through effective team building.

May this week of affirmations contribute to a workplace where team building flourishes, creating a resilient and collaborative environment.

Chapter 16

<u>Cultivating Change</u>: A Week of
Affirmations for Workplace Transformation

Monday (I Am):
I am a catalyst for positive change, leading
the way in transforming the workplace
environment.

Tuesday (I Have):
I have the resilience and adaptability
needed for workplace transformation,
embracing growth.

Wednesday (I Feel):
I feel the energy of positive transformation,
inspiring a renewed sense of purpose in the
workplace.

Thursday (I See):
I see opportunities for innovation and improvement, contributing to the ongoing workplace transformation.

Friday (I Speak):
I speak words of encouragement and forward-thinking, fostering a culture of positive workplace transformation.

Saturday (I Do):
I actively engage in actions that propel workplace transformation, encouraging a mindset of continuous improvement.

Sunday (I Create):
I create an environment that thrives on positive change, ensuring workplace transformation leads to lasting success.

May this week of affirmations guide you on a journey of positive workplace transformation and growth.

Chapter 17

<u>Serene Investments</u>: A Week of Affirmations for Cultivating Peace of Mind

Monday (I Am):
I am a mindful investor, approaching financial decisions with calmness and clarity.

Tuesday (I Have):
I have the knowledge and wisdom to make informed investment choices, promoting peace of mind.

Wednesday (I Feel):
I feel a sense of tranquility as I trust in my investment decisions and their long-term benefits.

Thursday (I See):
I see opportunities for financial growth, cultivating peace of mind through a strategic investment mindset.

Friday (I Speak):
I speak words of confidence and assurance, fostering a mindset that enhances peace in my financial endeavors.

Saturday (I Do):
I actively engage in actions that align with my financial goals, promoting peace of mind in my investments.

Sunday (I Create):
I create a harmonious relationship with my investments, ensuring lasting peace of mind in my financial journey.

May this week of affirmations bring peace and tranquility to your investment decisions and financial well-being.

Chapter 18

Leadership Evolution: A Week of Affirmations for Growth in Management

Monday (I Am):
I am a capable leader, ready to embrace growth and development in my management role.

Tuesday (I Have):
I have the skills and insight needed to navigate challenges and foster growth in management.

Wednesday (I Feel):
I feel the energy of progress and leadership evolution, propelling me toward effective management growth.

Thursday (I See):
I see opportunities for improvement and innovation, driving growth in my management approach.

Friday (I Speak):
I speak words of encouragement and leadership, cultivating a culture of continuous growth in management.

Saturday (I Do):
I actively engage in actions that contribute to my professional development and stimulate growth in management.

Sunday (I Create):
I create a vision for leadership evolution, ensuring a path of sustained growth in my management role.

May this week of affirmations inspire and guide you toward continuous growth and success in your management journey.

Chapter 19

Career Mastery: A Week of Affirmations for Professional Development

Monday (I Am):
I am a ifelong learner, committed to continuous professional development and growth.

Tuesday (I Have):
I have the resources and determination to invest in my professional development journey.

Wednesday (I Feel):
I feel the excitement of expanding my skills and knowledge, propelling me towards career mastery.

Thursday (I See):
I see challenges as opportunities for learning and professional development, embracing growth.

Friday (I Speak):
I speak words of ambition and self-improvement, fostering a culture of continuous professional development.

Saturday (I Do):
I actively engage in actions that contribute to my ongoing professional development, striving for excellence.

Sunday (I Create):
I create a roadmap for career mastery, ensuring a path of sustained professional development.

May this week of affirmations inspire and guide you on a fulfilling journey of continuous professional development and success.

Chapter 20

Unleashing Potential: A Week of
Affirmations for Personal Development

Monday (I Am):
I am a constant work in progress,
embracing the journey of personal
development.

Tuesday (I Have):
I have the resources and resilience to fuel
my personal growth and development.

Wednesday (I Feel):
I feel the power of transformation within,
propelling me towards continuous personal
development.

Thursday (I See):
I see challenges as stepping stones for
personal growth, recognizing the lessons in
every experience.   46

Friday (I Speak):
I speak words of self-improvement and empowerment, nurturing a mindset focused on personal development.

Saturday (I Do):
I actively engage in activities that contribute to my personal growth and development.

Sunday (I Create):
I create a life of continuous learning and improvement, prioritizing my personal development journey.

May this week of affirmations inspire and guide you on your path of personal development and self-discovery.

Chapter 21

<u>Innovative Ventures</u>: A Week of Affirmations for Business Innovation

Monday (I Am):
I am a creative force within my business, constantly fostering an environment of innovation.

Tuesday (I Have):
I have the insights and skills to drive business innovation, pushing the boundaries of what's possible.

Wednesday (I Feel):
I feel the energy of creativity flowing through my business, inspiring a culture of innovation.

Thursday (I See):
I see opportunities for groundbreaking
ideas and advancements, fueling business
innovation.

Friday (I Speak):
I speak words of encouragement and
forward-thinking, promoting a mindset of
continuous business innovation.

Saturday (I Do):
I actively engage in actions that encourage
experimentation and out-of-the-box
thinking, fostering business innovation.

Sunday (I Create):
I create a business culture that thrives on
innovation, ensuring sustained success
through groundbreaking ideas.

May this week of affirmations guide you
toward a business landscape filled with
creativity, innovation, and continuous
improvement.

Chapter 22

Innovative Synergy: A Week of Affirmations for Cultivating Creativity in the Workplace

Monday (I Am):
I am a catalyst for creativity, inspiring and fostering an environment of innovation in the workplace.

Tuesday (I Have):
I have the ability to tap into my creative potential and encourage others to do the same in the workplace.

Wednesday (I Feel):
I feel the vibrancy of creativity, infusing energy into every corner of the workplace.

Thursday (I See):
I see possibilities for creative solutions and ideas, sparking a culture of inventive thinking.

Friday (I Speak):
I speak words that encourage and celebrate creativity, fostering an atmosphere of open-mindedness.

Saturday (I Do):
I actively engage in activities that stimulate creativ ty, encouraging a culture of experimentation and fresh ideas.

Sunday (I Create):
I create an environment that nurtures and celebrates creativity, ensuring a workplace filled with innovative synergy.

May this week of affirmations contribute to a workplace where creativity flourishes, bringing forth fresh ideas and solutions.

51

Chapter 23

<u>Conclusion</u>

In the end, You win.